Telling th

Age 5-6

Melissa Blackwood, Liz Dawson & Stephen Monaghan

In a strange place, not too far from here, lives a scare of monsters.

A 'scare' is what some people call a group of monsters, but these monsters are really very friendly once you get to know them.

They are a curious bunch – they look very unusual, but they are quite like you and me, and they love learning new things and having fun.

In this book you will go on a learning journey with the monsters and you are sure to have lots of fun along the way.

Visit our website to meet the monsters and upload your drawings to the Monster Gallery.

Contents

Days of the Week

Grandpa is teaching Poggo about the days of the week. There are 7 days in 1 week and they come in this order:

Monday
Tuesday
Wednesday — weekdays
Thursday
Friday
Saturday — weekend
Sunday

Poggo goes to school on weekdays.

1 Help Poggo to write the names of the days.

Weekdays	Weekend
•	•
•	•
•	
•	
•	

2 Poggo has some fridge magnets.
Each has a day of the week on.
Write the days that are missing in the spaces.

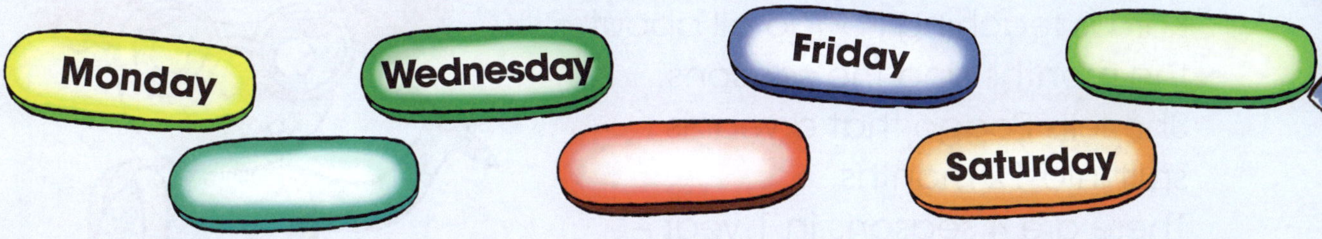

3 Answer these questions about the days of the week.

a It is Tuesday.
Which day comes **next**? ______________________

b It is Saturday.
Which day comes **next**? ______________________

c It is Wednesday.
What day was it **yesterday**? ______________________

d It is Sunday.
Which day comes **next**? ______________________

Fun Zone!

Join the dots to find out which animal is hiding.

Well done!
You can now find and colour **Shape 1** on the Monster Match page!

Months and Seasons

Kora is teaching Poggo all about the months and the seasons.
She tells Poggo that a year is split into 12 months.
There are 4 seasons in 1 year – Spring, Summer, Autumn and Winter.
Each season has 3 months in it.

January is the first month of the year.

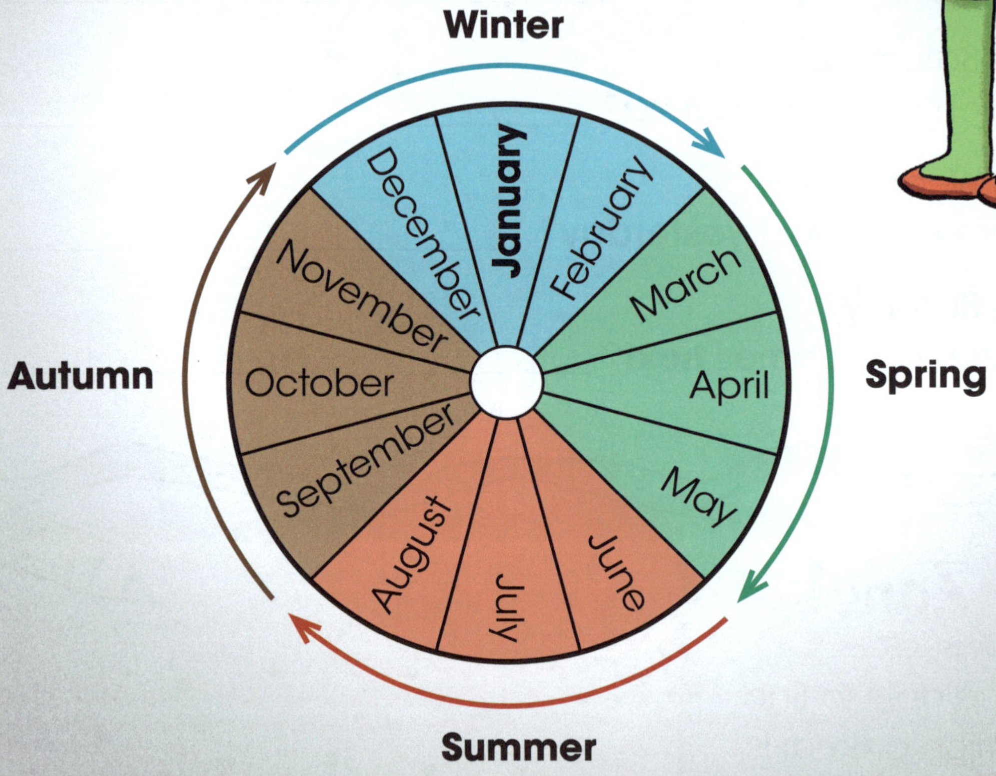

1 Help Poggo fill in the gaps in these sentences.

a There are ________________ months in Summer.

b There are ________________ seasons in a year.

c June is in the season of ________________.

2 Fill in the gaps in the sentences below. They are all about you!

a My birthday is in ______________ ,

which is in the season of ______________.

b My favourite season is ______________.

3 Write in the missing months of the year.

January	July
February	August
a ______________	**c** ______________
April	October
May	**d** ______________
b ______________	December

Fun Zone!

Make your own monster.

Looking scary! You can now find and colour **Shape 2** on the Monster Match page!

Monster Alien

You will need a see-through plastic cup, two paper bowls, coloured paper, white paper, a black crayon, paint, scissors and glue.

Ask an adult to help when needed.

1. Decorate the outside of your bowls with colourful paint and leave to dry. Glue the two tops of the bowls together.
2. Cut out two circles of white paper and draw a dot in the middle of each circle with the black crayon.
3. Scrunch the coloured paper and fill your plastic cup with it. Add two googly eyes.
4. Glue your plastic cup on top of the bowl.
5. Now you have a colourful monster alien!

Time Words

I am going to help Poggo understand these words that describe time.

quicker **slower** **earlier** **later**

I showed Poggo a picture of a snail and a racing car on the start line of a race.

Which do you think will be **quicker** in the race, the snail or the car?
Which will be **slower**?
Which will finish the race **earlier**?
Which will finish the race **later**?

The car will be **quicker**.
The snail will be **slower**.
The car will finish the race **earlier**.
The snail will finish the race **later**.

1 Help Poggo solve these problems using the time words. Look at the pictures and then fill in the answers.

a Who is **quicker** here?
Poggo or Kora?

__________________ is **quicker**.

b Who is **slower** here?
Poggo or Fizz?

__________________ is **slower**.

c Who is **quicker** here?
Fizz, Poggo or Gran?

____________________ is **quicker**.

2 Look at the pictures and tick the correct answers.

a Which happens **earlier** in the day, breakfast or lunch?

Breakfast ☐ Lunch ☐

b Which do you do **later** in the day, wake up or eat your lunch?

Wake up ☐ Eat lunch ☐

Fun Zone!

Make flowers out of paper.

Excellent!
You can now find and colour **Shape 3** on the Monster Match page!

Tissue Flowers

You will need coloured tissue paper, some stiff black card cut into a small circle, glue, a cup and a straw.

Ask an adult to help when needed.

1. Scrunch your tissue paper into lovely petal shapes. Use any colours you want.
2. Glue the tissue petals onto a black piece of card.
3. Attach your straw to make a stem.
4. Stand your flower in a cup.

How Long is a Second?

Webber is timing how long it takes to do different activities.
He uses his pocket watch to do this.
Webber's watch has a second hand that ticks around very quickly.
It is the red, thin hand on the watch.

Seconds tick past every little mark on the face of the watch, and are counted in ones.
When you have said '1 monster', a second has passed.
It takes 10 seconds for Webber to tie his shoelaces.

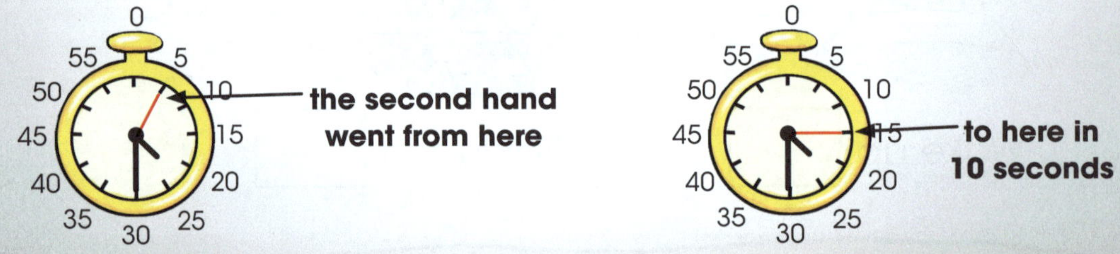

1 Work out how long it takes Webber to complete the following activities.
Write the number of seconds in the boxes.

a Polish a vase.

☐ seconds

b Pick a bunch of flowers.

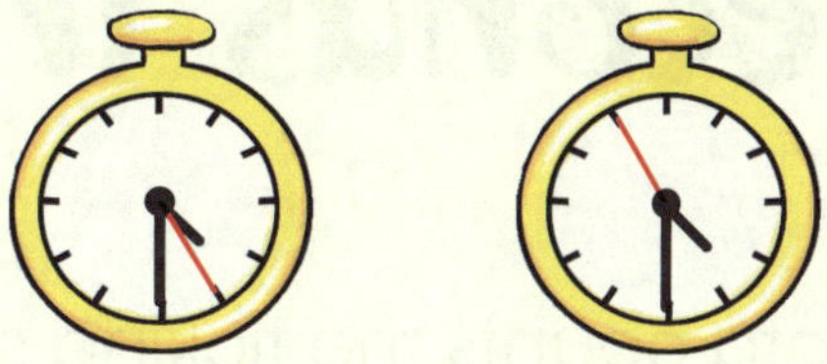

☐ seconds

c Fasten the buttons on his coat.

☐ seconds

2 In question 1, which activity took the most time? Write a, b or c in the box.

☐

Fun Zone!

Timer challenge! Ask an adult to time you with a watch to see how many seconds you can stand on one leg for. Record the number of seconds in the table. See if you can beat your score tomorrow.

Day	Number of seconds

Brilliant! You can now find and colour **Shape 4** on the Monster Match page!

Seconds in One Minute

Kora counts the ticking second hand of her watch.
The second hand has gone all the way around the watch face and back to the top by the time she has counted to 60.

Kora asks Mr Pepper if she has counted correctly.
Mr Pepper tells Kora that she is right and that there are **60 seconds in 1 minute**.

1 Kora uses the second hand on her watch to time how long it takes for Fizz and Tizz to run around the field at school.
It takes Fizz 17 seconds.
It takes Tizz 21 seconds.
Who is faster?

__________________ is faster.

2 Zak starts eating his dinner at exactly 5 o'clock.
Kora counts 18 seconds for Zak to eat his dinner.
Draw where the second hand finished on the watch face.

3 Kora uses the second hand on her watch to time how long it takes for Poggo to skateboard around the playground.

Lap	Time
1	35 seconds
2	28 seconds
3	36 seconds

a Which was Poggo's **fastest** lap?
Write the number of the lap in the box.

Lap ☐

b Which was Poggo's **slowest** lap?
Write the number of the lap in the box.

Lap ☐

c What is the **difference** between Poggo's fastest lap and slowest lap?
Write the number of seconds difference in the box.

☐ seconds

Fun Zone!

Have some hop scotch fun.

Fantastic!
You can now find and colour **Shape 5** on the Monster Match page!

Crazy Hop Scotch

You will need chalk, a small pebble and a place to draw on the ground outside – a patio or pavement is perfect.

Ask an adult to help when needed.

1. Draw 10 squares that join together.
2. Write the numbers 1 to 10 inside the squares.
3. Gently toss the pebble onto the squares.
4. You need to jump or hop over the square the pebble lands in.
5. To make the game harder, mix up the order of the numbers – you still have to hop or jump on the numbers in the right order!

O'clock

Grandpa tells Poggo that there are two hands on a clock.

The hour hand tells us what hour it is. The hour hand is the **little** hand (the red hand below).

The minute hand tells us how many minutes there are before the hour or after the hour.
The minute hand is the **big** hand (the blue hand below).

This kind of clock is an **analogue clock**.

It is 3 o'clock on this clock because the hour hand is pointing to 3 and the minute hand is pointing to the 12.
No minutes have passed after the hour.

Grandpa tells Poggo that 3 o'clock can also look like this.

This kind of clock is a **digital clock**.

1 Help Poggo tell the time on these clocks.
Write the times in the boxes.

a

It is ☐ o'clock.

b

It is ☐ o'clock.

c

It is ☐ o'clock.

2 Now help Poggo tell the time on these digital clocks. Write the times in the boxes.

a

It is ☐ o'clock.

b

It is ☐ o'clock.

c

It is ☐ o'clock.

3 Draw a line from each clock to the correct time.

10 o'clock	4 o'clock	12 o'clock

Fun Zone!

Find the five differences between these pictures of Poggo.

Good job!
You can now find and colour **Shape 6** on the Monster Match page!

How Long is an Hour?

An hour is made up of 60 minutes. When the minute hand has gone all the way around the clock, the hour hand will have moved on to the next number.

Otto is making a robot.
He waits an hour for the glue to dry before painting the robot.

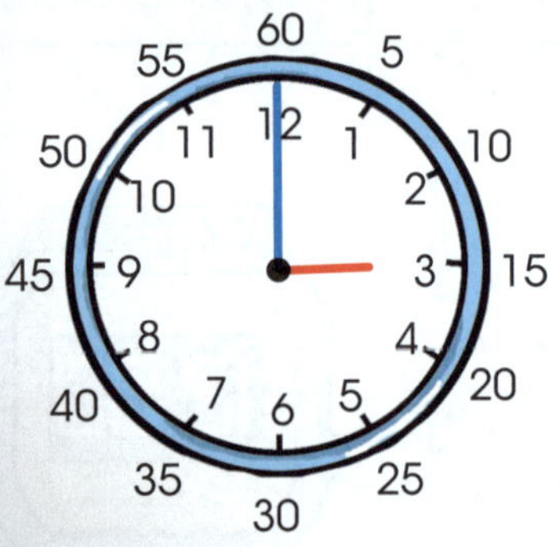

It is 3 o'clock.
Otto knows that the glue will be dry at 4 o'clock.

1 Circle the clock that shows 4 o'clock.

2 Otto has painted the robot and it is now 5 o'clock.

He needs to wait an hour before he can put the lights on the robot.

Draw the hour hand on the clock face to show 5 o'clock.

3 Otto has put the flashing lights on his robot and it is now 6 o'clock.

Otto needs to wait one more hour for the robot's batteries to charge up.

Draw the hour hand on the clock to show the time the robot will be ready to play with.

Fun Zone!

Find the time words in this word search. Words can go up, down, across and diagonally.

Super!
You can now find and colour **Shape 7** on the Monster Match page!

HOUR
MINUTE
MONTH
YEAR
DAY
SECOND
WEEK

S	E	C	O	N	D
K	H	K	D	S	M
E	O	W	Y	A	E
E	U	R	A	E	Y
W	R	Y	R	W	H
Y	H	T	N	O	M
M	I	N	U	T	E

Monster Challenge 1

1 Answer these questions about the days of the week.

a Which day comes after Monday?

____

b Which day is before Friday?

____

2 Answer these questions about the months of the year.

a Fill in the missing month.

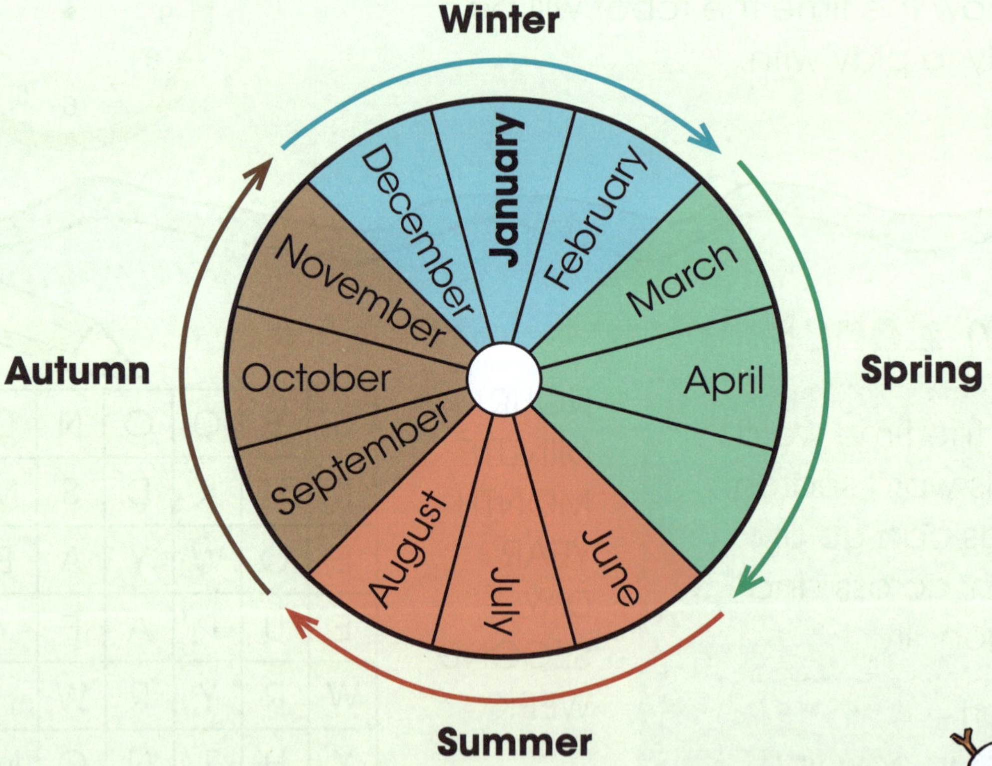

b Which season do you build a snowman in?

____

3 Answer these questions about time.

a There are ______________________ seconds in a minute.

b There are ______________________ minutes in an hour.

c What do you notice about the answers to **a** and **b**?

____

4 **a** What is the difference in hours between these two watches?

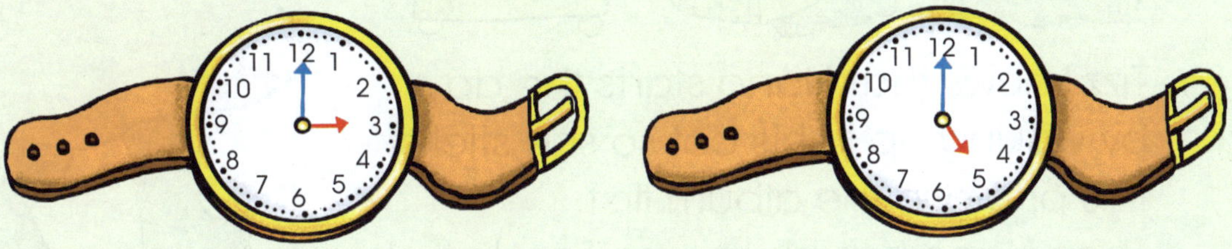

_______ hours

b What is the difference in hours between these two watches?

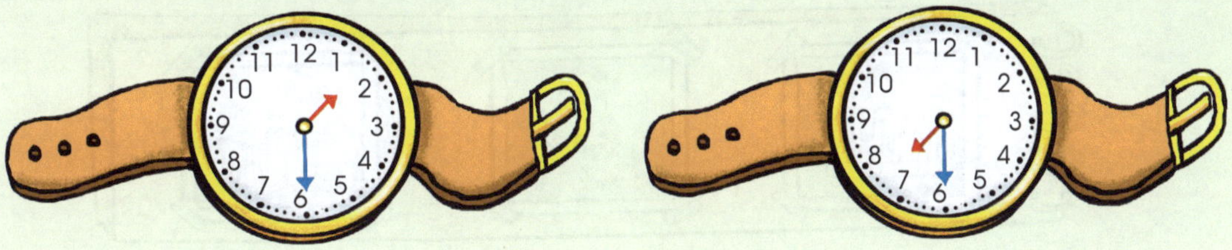

_______ hours

5 Here are the results of Noo's skipping challenge.
Noo tried three times to see **how long** she could keep skipping.

Try	Time
1	48 seconds
2	49 seconds
3	16 seconds

Write the number of Noo's **best** try in the box. ☐

Order of Events

Tizz has taken some photos of Nano to show Gran. She wants to make a book about Nano's day.

Tizz knows that Nano starts the day by waking up in his cot so she sticks this photo in the album first.
Then Nano has his milk so Tizz sticks this photo in next.
At the end of the day Mum reads Nano a bedtime story so she sticks this photo in last.

1 Help Tizz put these events in order.
Write a number 1 in the box next to the event that would happen first.
Write a number 2 in the box next to the event that would happen second.
Fill in all the boxes in order.

 ☐

 ☐

 ☐

2 Which of these activities is a day activity?
Which of these activities is a night activity?
'Getting changed' is both a day and a night activity, so it goes in the middle.
Write the activities in the correct sections.

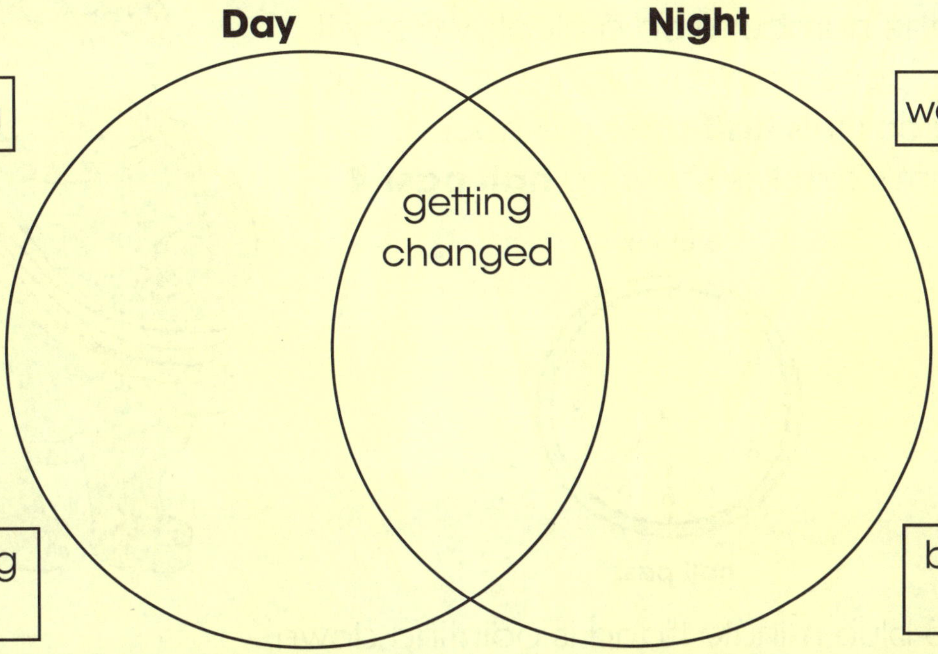

sleeping

waking up

brushing teeth

bedtime story

going to school

eating breakfast

Fun Zone!

Shout 'yo-ho-ho' in your pirate hat.

Monsterific! You can now find and colour **Shape 8** on the Monster Match page!

Pirate Hat

You will need a large sheet of newspaper. Ask an adult to help when needed.

1 Fold the sheet of newspaper in half.

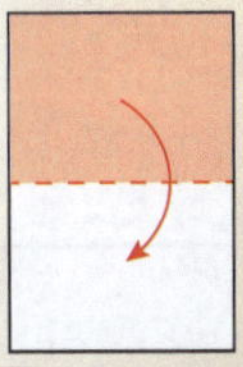

2 Fold the top corners down towards the centre of the page.

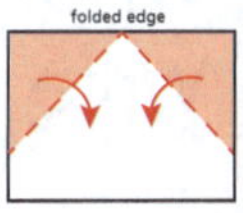

3 Lift the front flap at the bottom and fold it up.

4 Flip the paper over, then lift the bottom flap and fold it up.

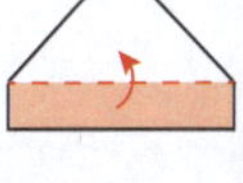

Half Past the Hour

Mum is explaining to Poggo that when the blue minute hand is pointing at the number 6 on a clock, we say it has gone half way around the clock. We call this **half past** the hour. Mum's clock is showing **half past 4**.

The blue minute hand is pointing down, and the red hour hand is pointing half way between the numbers 4 and 5. The red hour hand has gone **half way past 4**.

1 What time is it on these clocks? Write the answers on the lines.

a

____

b

____

2 Mum has given Poggo an old clock to practise moving the hands on. Help Poggo by drawing the hands on these clocks to show the correct times.

a

Half past 3

b

Half past 8

c

Half past 10

d

Half past 12

Fun Zone!

Make a monster noise.

Congratulations! You can now find and colour **Shape 9** on the Monster Match page!

Shaker Fun

You will need a clean, dry bottle with a lid, different dried seeds or beads to put inside the bottle, coloured paper and glue.

Ask an adult to help when needed.

1. Put some of the seeds or beads inside the bottle and put the lid on.
2. Use the coloured paper to cut some shapes and glue these on the bottle.
3. When the glue is dry, enjoy shaking your new instrument!

Quarter Past & Quarter To

Dad is helping Poggo figure out **quarter past** the hour and **quarter to** the hour.

There are two main parts to a clock.

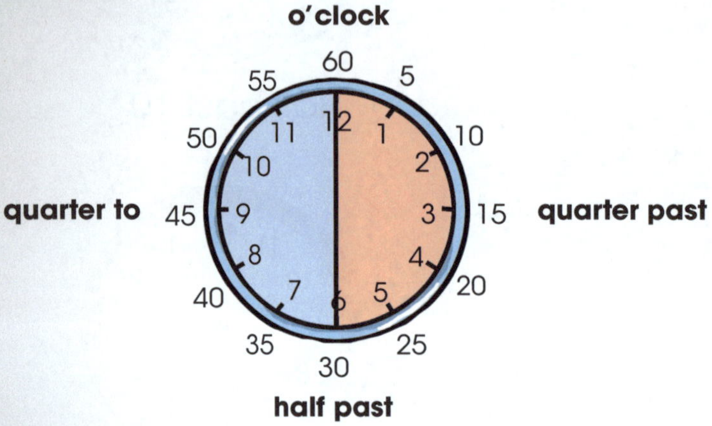

The blue side is '**to**' the hour.
The red side is '**past**' the hour.

If the long hand points to the **3**, it is **quarter past**.

If the long hand points to the **9**, it is **quarter to**.

1 Write down if the clocks show quarter past or quarter to the hour.

a

Quarter ________

b

Quarter ________

c

Quarter ________

2 Poggo is practising moving the hands on a clock with Dad. Help Poggo by drawing the hands on these clocks.

a

Quarter past 3

c

Quarter to 3

b

Quarter to 5

d

Quarter past 5

Fun Zone!

Make party glasses.

Splendid! You can now find and colour **Shape 10** on the Monster Match page!

Monster Glasses

You will need card or paper, scissors, glue, a pencil, things to decorate your glasses: glitter, stickers, etc.

Ask an adult to help when needed.

1. Draw your glasses on card or paper.
2. Cut them out.
3. Decorate your glasses to make them jazzy.

5 Minute Intervals

Fizz is usually 5 minutes late for everything the monsters do!

Each number on the clock is spaced apart by 5 minutes.
When the minute hand has moved 1 number, 5 minutes have passed.
2 numbers = 10 minutes
3 numbers = 15 minutes, and so on.

The monsters are having a disco.
The disco starts at **1.30**.
Tizz looks at the clock when the disco starts.
She knows that Fizz will turn up 5 minutes later, at **1.35**.

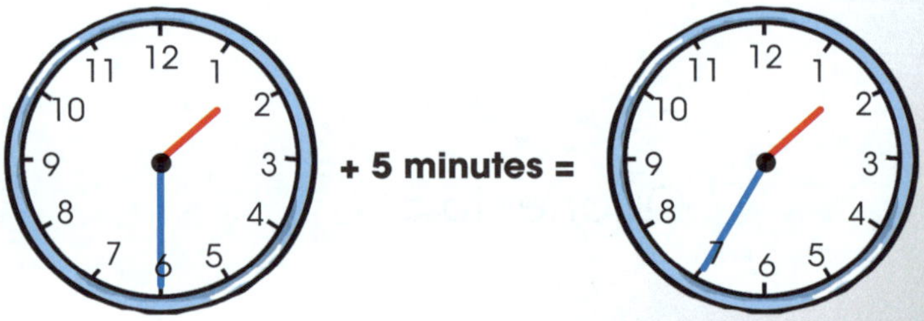

1.30 **1.35**

1 Draw the hands on the clocks to show when Fizz will arrive.
Write on the answer lines when Fizz will arrive.

a The monster picnic starts at 12.
Fizz is **5 minutes late**.

Fizz will arrive at __________.

b The monster skate festival starts at 3.45.
Fizz is **5 minutes late**.

Fizz will arrive at __________.

2 Draw the hands on the clocks to show when Tizz will arrive.
Write on the answer lines when Tizz will arrive.

a The monster concert starts at 2.30.
Tizz is **10 minutes early**.

Tizz will arrive at __________.

b The monster movie will start at 12.25.
Tizz is **10 minutes early**.

Tizz will arrive at __________.

Fun Zone!

Make a crown out of a paper plate.

Well done!
You can now find and colour **Shape 11** on the Monster Match page!

Paper Plate Crown

You will need a paper plate, paint, a pencil, a ruler and a pair of scissors.

Ask an adult to help when needed.

1. Fold the paper plate in half.
2. Draw lines on the back of the half plate to divide it into quarters. Don't draw the lines all the way to the edge of the plate.
3. Cut along the four dividing lines, stopping about 2 centimetres from the edge.
4. Flatten the plate out and decorate the back with paint.
5. Push the cut sections of the plate up and out to the make the sides of the crown.

Time Word Problems

Kora and Poggo are timing how long the monsters take to do things. Poggo and Kora want to know how long it takes Mum to wash the car. They use the analogue clock to help them find out.

start

finish

Mum starts to wash the car at **2 o'clock**.
It takes Mum until **3.30** to wash the car.

Using the analogue clock, Kora and Poggo know that it takes Mum **1 hour and 30 minutes** to wash the car.

1 Help Poggo and Kora work out the end time that each monster finishes a job.

a Dad starts mowing the lawn at 3 o'clock.
It takes him 2 hours to mow the lawn.
Draw the start and finish times on the clocks.

Start

Finish

b Litmus finishes an experiment at 4 o'clock.
It took him 3 hours to finish the experiment.
Draw the start and finish times on the clocks.

Start

Finish

2 Use the clocks in question 1 to help you work out these problems.

a Kora goes to the cinema at 1 o'clock.
She comes home at 4 o'clock.
How long was she at the cinema for?

____

b Litmus visits a science exhibition at 2 o'clock.
He comes home at 7 o'clock.
How long was Litmus away for?

____

Fun Zone!

Catch the light with a glitter bottle.

Awesome!
You can now find and colour **Shape 12** on the Monster Match page!

Glitter Bottle

You will need a water bottle with a lid, glitter and water.

Ask an adult to help when needed.

1. Put some glitter into a water bottle.
2. Fill the bottle up with water.
3. Close the bottle and shake.
4. Put your glitter bottle on a windowsill in the sun. See how it changes colour as the light passes through it.

Monster Challenge 2

1 Circle all of the activities that are done in the morning.

eating breakfast

going to school

going to bed

leaving school

waking up

2 Write the time in words on the answer line.

______________ ______________ ______________

3 What times do these clocks show?
Write your answers in words.

______________ ______________ ______________

4 What times do these clocks show?
Write your answers in words.

______________ ______________

5 What times do these clocks show?
Write your answers in words.

______________ ______________

I knew you could do it!
You have made it to the end of the book.
You are a magnificent monster!

Answers

Page 2

1 **Weekdays**
- Monday
- Tuesday
- Wednesday
- Thursday
- Friday

Weekend
- Saturday
- Sunday

Page 3

2 Tuesday, Thursday and Sunday are missing

3 **a** Wednesday
b Sunday
c Tuesday
d Monday

Fun Zone!

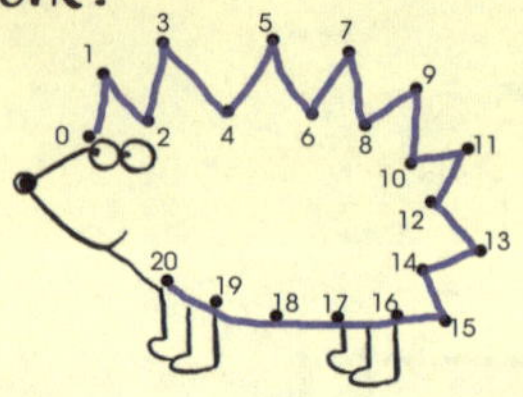

Page 4

1 **a** There are 3 months in Summer.
b There are 4 seasons in a year.
c June is in the season of Summer.

Page 5

2 **a** Child to fill in their birthday month and the season it is in
b Child to fill in their favourite season

3 **a** March
b June
c September
d November

Page 6

1 **a** Kora
b Fizz

Page 7

c Fizz

2 **a** Breakfast
b Eat lunch

Page 8

1 **a** 15 seconds

Page 9

b 30 seconds
c 20 seconds

2 b

Page 10

1 Fizz

2

Page 11

3 **a** Lap 2
b Lap 3
c 8 seconds

Page 12

1 **a** 8 o'clock
b 10 o'clock
c 5 o'clock

Page 13

2 **a** 2 o'clock
b 7 o'clock
c 11 o'clock

3

Fun Zone!

Page 14

1 Third clock should be circled

Page 15

2

3

Fun Zone!

S	E	C	O	N	D
K	H	K	D	S	M
E	O	W	Y	A	E
E	U	R	A	E	Y
W	R	Y	R	W	H
Y	H	T	N	O	M
M	I	N	U	T	E

Page 16

1 **a** Tuesday
b Thursday

2 **a** May
b Winter

Page 17

3 **a** 60
b 60
c They are both the same

4 **a** 2 hours
b 6 hours

5 2

Page 18

1

Page 19

2

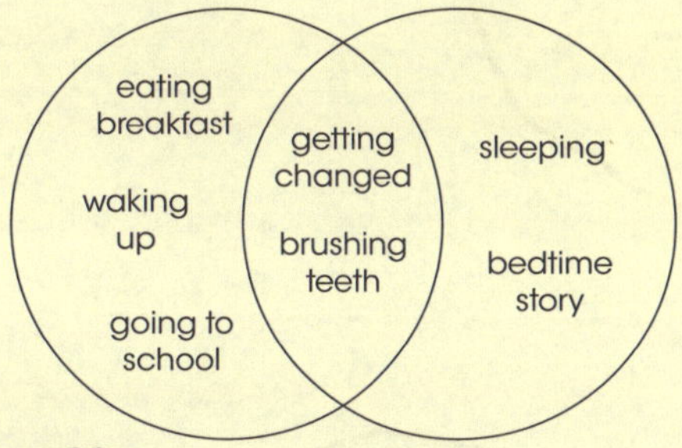

Page 20

1 **a** Half past 2
b Half past 11

Page 21

2 **a**

c

b

d

Page 22

1 **a** Quarter to
b Quarter past
c Quarter to

Page 23

2 **a**

c

b

d

Page 24

1 **a** Fizz will arrive at 12.05.

b Fizz will arrive at 3.50.

Page 25

2 **a** Tizz will arrive at 2.20.

b Tizz will arrive at 12.15.

Page 26

1 **a**

Start

Finish

Page 27

b

Start

Finish

2 **a** 3 hours
b 5 hours

Page 28

1 Waking up, going to school and eating breakfast should all be circled

2 9 o'clock, 8 o'clock, 12 o'clock

Page 29

3 Half past 3, half past 1, half past 12

4 Quarter to 8, quarter past 7

5 Ten past 4, twenty to 3

Monster Match

Each time you complete a topic in this book, you will be awarded a shape number.

Find and colour the shapes in the picture of the snowmonster that match the numbers you have been given.

As you work through the book you will gradually see the snowmonster come to life!